OCT   2004

SPAIN

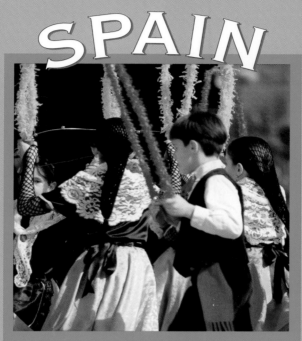

A TRUE BOOK®

by
Martin Hintz

Children's Press®
A Division of Scholastic Inc.

New York Toronto London Auckland Sydney
Mexico City New Delhi Hong Kong
Danbury, Connecticut

Puente Nuevo (New Bridge) in the historic town of Ronda

Reading Consultant
Sonja I. Smith
Reading Specialist

Content Consultant
Dr. Amy J. Johnson, Ph.D.
Berry College

Library of Congress Cataloging-in-Publication Data

Hintz, Martin.
    Spain / Martin Hintz.
        p. cm. — (A true book)
Includes bibliographical references and index.
Contents: Living on a peninsula—A glorious history—Making a new
Spain—People of Spain—Festive Spain.
    ISBN 0-516-22815-3 (lib. bdg.)   0-516-27930-0 (pbk.)
    1. Spain—Juvenile literature. [1. Spain.] I. Title. II. Series.
DP17.H56 2004
946—dc22
                                                          2003018664

CHILDREN'S PRESS, and A TRUE BOOK™, and associated logos are
trademarks and or registered trademarks of Scholastic Library Publishing.
SCHOLASTIC and associated logos are trademarks and or registered
trademarks of Scholastic Inc.
1 2 3 4 5 6 7 8 9 10 R 13 12 11 10 09 08 07 06 05 04

Contents

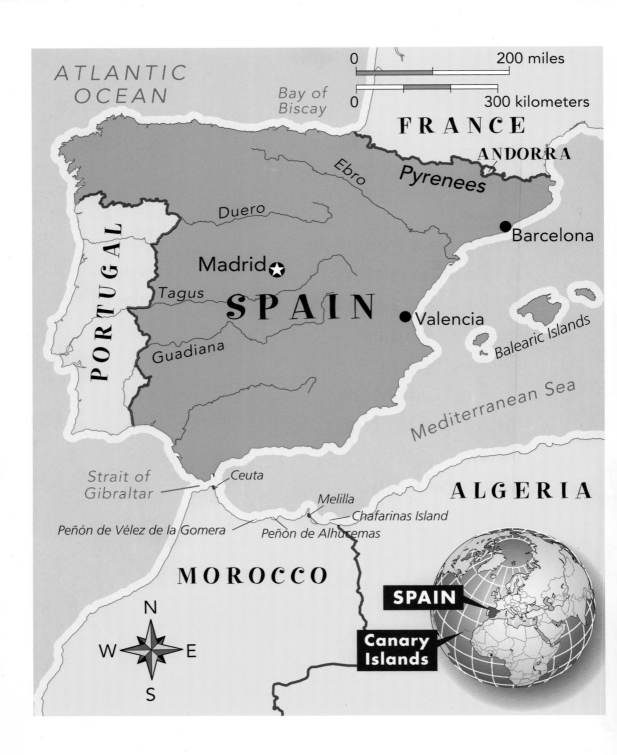

Living on a Peninsula

Spain is located on the Iberian **Peninsula** in the southwestern corner of Europe. It shares this tip of land with Portugal. Spain's northern neighbors are France and Andorra. They are separated from Spain by the jagged Pyrenees Mountains. To the south are the deep-blue waters of the Mediterranean Sea. To the northwest is the Bay of Biscay.

Spain is separated from Africa by the Strait of Gibraltar, a narrow body of water that separates the Mediterranean Sea and the Atlantic Ocean. The Canary Islands in the Atlantic Ocean and the Balearic Islands in the Mediterranean Sea are also part of Spain, as well as three small islands off Morocco's coast and two **enclaves** in North Africa.

A cactus growing on Tenerife, the largest of the Canary Islands (left); The high mountains of Spain (below)

Spain has a varied landscape with five major mountain ranges. These towering peaks make Spain the highest nation

The mountains of Spain are dotted with small villages (left). A flock of sheep roams the countryside in Castille (below).

in Europe after Switzerland. A large central **plateau** is surrounded by rugged hills.

Some of the countryside is rich and green. Other parts are dry and windblown. A small portion of Spain is covered with forests. There are also pastures, where sheep can graze.

The Tagus (Tajo), Guadiana, Duero, Río Mino, and Ebro are the mightiest rivers in Spain. Dams block several of these waterways. **Hydroelectric** or water-powered plants use the energy of moving water in these dammed rivers to produce electricity for homes and businesses.

9

Spain's crumbly, mineral-rich soil contributes to growing marvelous grapes that make fine red, white, and sparkling wines. Large groves of ancient trees produce delicious olives. These are pressed into excellent oil, which is sold around the world.

An olive tree grove

People enjoy the good weather at an outdoor café.

Spain can be very hot and dry in the summer. The winters can be cold and wet, especially in the north. Yet for much of the year, Spain's climate is pleasant. Friends can relax at outdoor cafés after work or school.

A Glorious History

Merchants from ancient cultures around the Mediterranean visited the Spanish peninsula to buy, sell, and trade goods. By 19 B.C., all of Spain had become a colony, or outpost, of the Romans. The Romans remained there for several hundred years. They built beautiful temples,

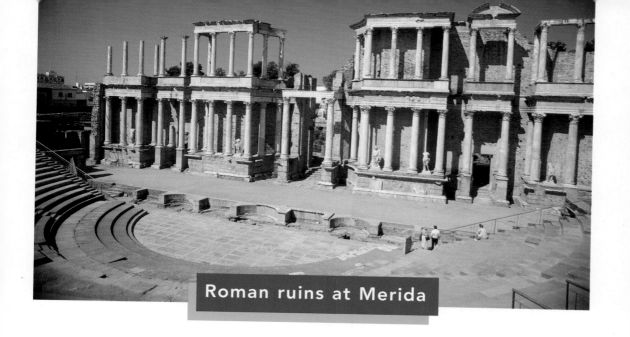

Roman ruins at Merida

amphitheaters, and baths that still exist today. After the Romans departed, various warlike people from northern Europe settled in Spain. Each left its mark on Spanish culture.

The Moors from Africa conquered most of Spain by

A.D. 719. They were a fierce, proud people who followed the Muslim faith. The Moors were noted for their knowledge of art and science. They built splendid cities like Cordoba, Toledo, and Seville. The rest of Christian Europe, however, feared the Moors because of their different religion and customs. Christian armies drove the last Moors from Spain in 1492.

With the Moors finally gone, Spain turned its attention to the rest of the world. Under Spanish

Christopher Columbus convinced Queen Isabella I and King Ferdinand V to pay for his voyage.

monarchs, or rulers, like Queen Isabella I and King Ferdinand V of Aragon, Spain became a great power. Brave adventurers such as Christopher Columbus were sent across the unmapped oceans to establish colonies far away from home. Tough Spanish soldiers such as Francisco Pizarro and Hernán Cortés conquered the Inca Empire in Peru and defeated the Aztecs in Mexico. Hernando de Soto explored lands from Florida to the Mississippi River. Francisco Vásquez de Coronado traveled through the American Southwest. Priests accompanied the armies. They carried the message of Christianity to the kingdom's newly acquired territories.

Coronado led an expedition of more than 1,000 people through the American Southwest.

From the 1500s to the 1700s, resources taken from its colonies made Spain very rich. Valuable minerals and exotic foods such as potatoes, corn, and tobacco were brought to Spain from these distant lands. Merchant

Spanish merchant ships carried the riches of the New World back to Spain.

ships called galleons carried gold, silver, and precious stones back to Spain from America. However, terrible storms often wrecked the lumbering vessels. Treasure hunters still seek the remains of these long-ago ships.

Making a New Spain

After the reign of Queen Isabella I, Spain fought a series of bloody wars with its neighbors throughout the 1700s and 1800s. These countries battled over who would control trade routes or colonies. It became very difficult to protect Spain's farflung territories. Some were

captured by other countries or lost through revolutions by the people who lived there. As a result, Spain gradually lost its influence abroad. In 1898, Spain was defeated by the

United States in the Spanish-American War, and Spain had to give up most of its few remaining colonies. Among them were Cuba and the Philippines.

Following political unrest at home, King Alfonso XIII left the country in 1931. A republic was formed in which the Spanish people could elect their own leaders. However, not all of the Spanish people wanted the king to leave. This resulted in

Armored cars arrive in Madrid during the Spanish Civil War.

a terrible civil war that lasted from 1936 to 1939. Thousands of people were killed, buildings were destroyed, and crops were ruined by the fighting. Enemies of the king eventually won, led by General Francisco Franco. He was a dictator, a ruler with absolute power who controlled Spain with an iron fist until he died.

At the death of Franco, the **monarchy** was restored. Control of the country went to King Juan Carlos, Alfonso's grandson. He quickly reformed the government

King Juan Carlos

and made it more responsive
to the people. The country is
now a **parliamentary** monarchy,
with the king as head of state.
The prime minister handles the

Lawmakers meet in Madrid.

day-to-day running of the government. The National Assembly,
consisting of a Senate and
Congress of Deputies, passes
laws. All of the national politicians
meet in the capital city of Madrid
to conduct business.

People of Spain

With more than 40 million residents, Spain is Europe's fifth most populous nation. The people are a wonderful mix of the many cultures that have called Spain their home over the centuries.

The Basques are a distinctive group with their own customs.

Most live along the mountain-ous border with France. They speak Spanish, but they also have their own language, called Euskara. Some Basques

A group of Basques protests the use of violence to gain independence.

want total independence from Spanish authority. A few support the use of violence to achieve their aims, but most Basques pursue their goals in a peaceful manner.

Barcelona, Madrid, and Valencia are the most heavily populated areas in Spain. Many Spaniards are still farmers, yet a growing number of young people have moved to the cities to work in the computer and service industries. Spain's other major businesses include tourism and chemical manufacturing.

The country also takes its international responsibilities seriously. It belongs to such organizations as the European Union and the United Nations. These groups help with relief efforts in poorer parts of the world. They also provide peacekeeping

Pablo Picasso

Along with El Greco (1541–1614) and Francisco José de Goya (1746–1828), Pablo Picasso (1881–1973) was among Spain's most famous artists. Son of a Basque drawing teacher, Picasso studied in Barcelona and Madrid. His first art show was in 1901 in Paris.

Picasso's paintings are bold, colorful, and vibrant. One of his most famous paintings is *Guernica*. It depicts an air attack during the Spanish Civil War. Picasso produced hundreds of works of art now shown in museums and private collections throughout the world. His exhibitions always draw large crowds of art lovers. His paintings are very valuable.

Pablo Picasso at work

soldiers in regions where war might break out.

Spain has a great **literary** history. Many of its authors have won international prizes. One of the country's best-known works of fiction is the novel Don Quixote, written by Miguel de Cervantes (1547–1616). The famous story tells of a kindly gentleman who thinks he is a knight and goes out to right what he sees are the wrongs of the world.

A painting of Don Quixote
by Jacques Neilson

Many Spanish people love sports, especially soccer, or fútbol. Spain's many talented players make for exciting games. Spaniards also love hiking and bicycling along the

country's back roads and along its trails. The waters off the country's sun-drenched beaches offer excellent swimming. Surfers flock to the coastline to catch a ride on a wild wave.

Festive Spain

The Spanish enjoy parades and parties on their public holidays. National Day on October 12 celebrates the country's freedom. It marks the day when explorer Christopher Columbus reached the New World. Spain's constitution is honored on Constitution Day, December 6.

Spanish soldiers march in a National Day parade.

On these days, school is out, and most adults have a day off from work.

Christmas decorations in Madrid

More than 90 percent of the population consider themselves Roman Catholics, so the Christmas season is one of the most festive times of the year in Spain. Many homes and town squares exhibit a large nativity scene, called the nacimiento. Villages hold Christmas markets where vendors sell toys, candy, chestnuts, and delicious apples.

Bullfighting is a popular folk tradition in Spain. The fight is held in a large, sandy ring called the plaza de toros, the "place of the bulls." Fighting bulls are a

A matador, or bullfighter, uses his cape to control the bull.

special breed and are very fierce. The bullfighter, called a matador, lures the angry animal with elaborate cape movements. The kill is made with a sword. Famous bullfighters such as Manolete (1917–1947) are admired throughout the country.

Flamenco is a musical heritage that began in Spain's southern region of Andalusia. It is now heard throughout the country. The music is believed to have been developed by the Gypsies, a race of people from northwest

India. They appeared in Europe in the 1600s and still travel from place to place. Flamenco dancing involves stamping of the feet and vigorous hand clapping to the sound of a guitar.

A family in Barcelona enjoys a meal together.

Spanish families enjoy getting together and eating. Lunch is usually the main meal of the day. Much of Spanish **cuisine** on the coast features seafood such as eels, cod, and squid. Regional specialties in other parts of Spain include bean soup, cheeses, and

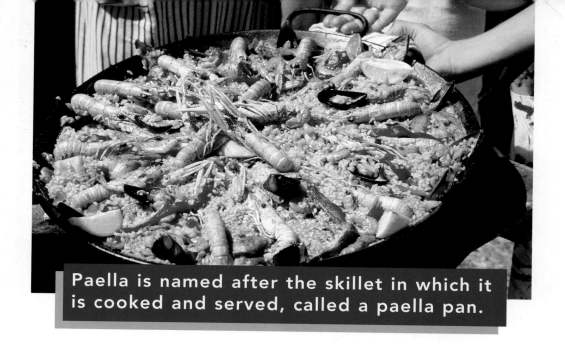

Paella is named after the skillet in which it is cooked and served, called a paella pan.

apple cider. Paella is another popular dish, made with rice, meat, and seafood. Spain is also noted for its many types of wine. When everyone is having a good time, Spaniards offer a toast and say, "A su salud!" This means "To your health!"

To Find Out More

Here are some additional resources to help you learn more about Spain:

 **Books**

Davis, Kevin. **Look What Came From Spain.** Franklin Watts, 2002.

Furlong, Kate A. **Spain.** ABDO Publishing Company/Checkerboard Library, 2003.

Lior, Noa, and Tara Steele. **Spain: The People.** Crabtree, 2001.

Molzahn, Arlene Bourgeois. **Christopher Columbus: Famous Explorer**. Enslow Publishers, 2003.

Venezia, Mike. **Getting to Know the World's Greatest Artists: Picasso**. Children's Press, 1988.

Organizations and Online Sites

National Tourist Office of Spain

666 Fifth Avenue
New York, NY 10103
212-265-8822
http://www.okspain.org

For updates on Spanish attractions and vacations, as well as things to see and do when visiting the country.

Spanish Monarchy

http://www.casareal.es/
casareal/home2i.html

This official web site of the Spanish royal family describes the monarchy, the crown, and the king's duties. It also shows the palaces and houses where the king and his family live.

All About Spain

http://www.red2000.com/
spain

For information about traveling in Spain, plus Spanish customs, holidays, and attractions.

Lonely Planet World Guide: Spain

http://www.lonelyplanet.com/
destinations/europe/spain

For details on the history, culture, environment, and events in Spain.

Spanish Vocabulary Builder

http://www.language
adventure.net

For basic Spanish words.

Important Words

amphitheater a large, open-air stadium where sports events and concerts are held

cuisine the style of cooking

enclave a small piece of land surrounded by another country

hydroelectric relating to the production of electricity by water power

literary relating to written works

monarchy a government headed by a king, queen, or emperor

parliamentary where a chosen group of people are responsible for making laws

peninsula a piece of land with water on three sides

plateau a level section of high ground

Index

Meet the Author

Martin Hintz lives in Milwaukee, Wisconsin. Hintz has written many books for Scholastic/Children's Press, including a number of award-winning cultural geographies in the Enchantment of the World and America the Beautiful series. He also writes for numerous magazines and newspapers. Hintz publishes The Irish American Post, an online news and features outlet about Irish culture and people.

Hintz has traveled throughout the world while researching his books. He spent summers working on road crews while he was in high school and college. He also worked for a railroad carnival that performed at many fairs and numerous festivals around the United States and in Canada. He has bachelor's and master's degrees in journalism, with an emphasis on international affairs.